KU-765-485

# Contents

Penguin relatives ................... 4

Where penguins live ........... 6

Finding food ..................... 8

Coming ashore ................. 10

Mating ............................. 12

Eggs ................................ 14

Babies ............................. 16

Growing up ..................... 18

Moulting .......................... 20

Emperor penguin facts ....... 22

Glossary .......................... 24

Index .............................. 24

Some words are shown in bold, **like this**. You can find out what they mean by looking in the glossary.

# Penguin relatives

chinstrap penguins

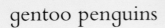

gentoo penguins

There are 17 different kinds of penguin.
They all live in the southern half of the
world. Penguins cannot fly, but they are
excellent swimmers. They are seabirds.

# Really WILD

# PENGUINS

Books are to be returned on or before
the last date below.

Dartford Library
Tel: 01322 221133
Fax: 01322 278271
dartfordlibrary@kent.gov.uk

02. JUL 08.

05. SEP 0?

04. OCT 08.

1 MAR 2009

SUM 8|15

25 SEP 2010

09 OCT 2010
04 NOV 2010

-5 JUN 2009
26 SEP 2009
25 JAN 2010
15 FEB 2010
15 FEB 2010
1 0 MAR 2010
14 AUG 2010

22 NOV 2010
9 NOV 2011

-1 MAY 2013

11 OCT 2016

30 AUG 2019

**LIBRARIES**    Penguins

CHARTER MARK
DARTFORD
Dartford 221133
**Awarded for excellence**

Kent
County
Council
ARTS & LIBRARIES

son

C090340966

KENT
ARTS & LIBRARIES

C90340966

First published in Great Britain by Heinemann Library
Halley Court, Jordan Hill, Oxford OX2 8EJ,
a division of Reed Educational and Professional Publishing Ltd.

OXFORD  FLORENCE  PRAGUE  MADRID  ATHENS
MELBOURNE  AUCKLAND  KUALA LUMPUR  SINGAPORE  TOKYO
IBADAN  NAIROBI  KAMPALA  JOHANNESBURG  GABORONE
PORTSMOUTH NH (USA)  CHICAGO  MEXICO CITY  SAO PAULO

© Reed Educational and Professional Publishing Ltd 1997

All rights reserved. No part of this publication may be reproduced, stored in a retrieval system,
or transmitted in any form or by any means, electronic, mechanical, photocopying, recording,
or otherwise without either the prior written permission of the Publishers or a licence permitting
restricted copying in the United Kingdom issued by the Copyright Licensing Agency Ltd,
90 Tottenham Court Road, London W1P 9HE

Designed by Celia Floyd
Illustrations by Alan Fraser (Pennant Illustration) and Hardlines (map p.6)
Colour reproduction by Dot Gradations.
Printed in Hong Kong / China

01 00 99 98
10 9 8 7 6 5 4 3 2 1

ISBN 0 431 02867 2

**British Library Cataloguing in Publication Data**

Robinson, Claire
Penguins. - (Really wild)
1. Penguins - Juvenile literature
I. Title
598.4'41

This book is also available in a hardback library edition (ISBN 0 431 02866 4).

Flick the pages of this book and see what happens!

**Acknowledgements**
The Publishers would like to thank the following for permission to reproduce photographs:
B & C Alexander/H. Reinhard, pp.7, 11, 12, 13;
Ardea London Ltd/Peter Steyn, p.4 bottom;
Bruce Coleman Ltd, p.5 top (Dr Eckart Pott), p.9 (Francisco J. Erize), p.10 (Hans Reinhard);
FLPA, p.4 top & p.20 (C. Carvalho), p.21 (M. Horning/Earthviews);
Oxford Scientific Films, p.5 bottom (Kjell Sandved); p.6 (Daniel Cox),
pp.8 & 22 (G. I. Kooyman), pp.14, 15, 16 & 18 (Doug Allan), p.17 (Colin Monteath),
p.19 (Konrad Wothe), p.23 (Kjell Sandved).
Cover photograph: Oxford Scientific Films/Kjell Sandved

Our thanks to Oxford Scientific Films for their help and co-operation in the preparation of
this book.

Every effort has been made to contact copyright holders of any material reproduced in this
book. Any omissions will be rectified in subsequent printings if notice is given to the Publisher.

rockhopper penguins

emperor penguins

Emperor penguins are the largest kind of penguin. Let's see how they live.

# Where penguins live

Emperor penguins live in the cold seas around **Antarctica**. This is a land covered in ice and snow.

The penguins spend most of the summer
in the water. They come ashore to **breed**
and **moult**.

# Finding food

The penguins are very fast and **agile** swimmers. When they want food, they dive deep in search of fish and **squid**.

There is danger in the sea. This leopard seal is a fierce hunter that eats penguins, but it can only catch them in the water!

# Coming ashore

It is autumn and the penguins come ashore to breed. They swim fast underwater towards the land. Then they shoot upwards and land on the ice.

Penguins can't walk fast. Sometimes they flop onto their tummies and push themselves along with their feet. This is called **tobogganing**. It is fun, and quick!

# Mating

The emperors are on their long autumn journey across the ice. They travel to the place where they lay their eggs each year.

Emperor penguins have the same partner for life. Now they find their partners after five months apart. They do a dance called a **mating display**.

# Eggs

After three weeks, the female lays one large egg. Then she **treks** back to sea to find food. The male guards the egg. He keeps it warm on his feet under a flap of skin.

It is freezing cold. The males all **huddle** together. They cannot feed because they are looking after the eggs, so they live off the fat in their bodies.

# Babies

Two months later the eggs hatch. The mothers return from the sea to care for the chicks. At last the hungry fathers are free to go off in search of food.

Emperor chicks are covered in **downy** grey feathers. After a few weeks, they are too big to sit on their mother's feet.

# Growing up

Both parents travel to and fro across the ice collecting food from the sea. This father feeds his growing chick with half-eaten fish.

The chicks grow up in large groups
watched over by adult penguins. There
are hundreds of them in the **rookery**.

# Moulting

As summer draws near, the young penguins **moult**. Shiny new feathers push out the old ones. Now the birds are waterproof and ready to swim.

The ice over the sea has melted.
The young penguins dive in for the first
time. Next year, if they live, they will
return here to moult.

# Emperor penguin facts

- Emperor penguins are the largest kind of penguin. They are over one metre tall.

- Their flipper-like wings are very powerful. They can dive deeper than most seabirds.

- Emperors can live for 20 years. They have their first chick when they are about five years old.

- Males and females look the same, but they make different sounds.

# Glossary

**agile**  quick and graceful
**Antarctica**  continent of mountains and ice at the southern tip of the world
**breed**  have babies
**downy**  soft and fluffy
**huddle**  keep very close together
**mating**  two animals making a baby together
**mating display**  a kind of dance that males and females do, before mating
**moult**  lose old feathers and grow new ones
**rookery**  a large group of penguins
**squid**  a sea animal with eight trailing arms
**tobogganing**  sliding across the snow
**trek**  make a difficult journey

# Index

chicks   4, 17, 18, 19, 21, 23
eggs   12, 14, 15, 16
feathers   17, 20
feeding   8, 15, 16, 18
females   14, 16, 17, 23
finding food   8, 16, 18

keeping warm   14, 15
males   14, 15, 16, 18, 23
moulting   7, 20, 21
swimming   4, 7, 8, 10, 20, 22
travelling   10, 11, 12, 14, 18